Don't Feed the Elephants! Workbook

Overcoming the Art of Avoidance to Build Powerful Partnerships

Sarah Noll Wilson
and
Dr. Teresa Peterson

Published by Eight Gables Press

Copyright © 2024 by Sarah Noll Wilson, Inc.

All Rights Reserved.

No part of this book may be used or reproduced by any means, graphic, electronic, or mechanical, including photocopying, recording, taping, or by any information storage retrieval system without the written permission of the authors or publisher except in the case of brief quotations embodied in critical articles and reviews.

ISBN: 979-8-9917431-1-2

Table of Contents

Welcome 5

How to Use This Workbook 9

Chapter 1   Signs There Might Be an Elephant in the Room 11

Chapter 2   This Is What Your Brain Is Doing on Stress 19

Chapter 3   Naming Your Elephants 27

Chapter 4   Are You Feeding the Elephant? 37

Chapter 5   Step One: Be Curious with Yourself 45

Chapter 6   Step Two: Be Curious about Others 55

Chapter 7   Step Three: Be Curious with Others 63

Chapter 8   All Together: Freeing the Elephant 75

Chapter 9   Receiving the Elephant: The Self-Awareness You Didn't Know You Needed 83

Chapter 10   Receiving the Elephant: Feedback, Intention, and Apologies – Oh My! 89

Chapter 11   When Freeing the Elephant Goes Differently than We'd Hoped 101

Chapter 12   Ready, Set, Act 111

Closing Thoughts 117

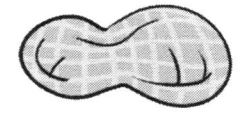

Welcome

"No one benefits from your caution, but many can benefit from your courage." – Minda Harts

A Journey Continues

"I know you wrote this for the workplace Sarah, but I have to tell you how valuable these strategies have been in talking with my spouse and family members. We have some serious elephants in my family."

Some version of this comment has been shared with me more times than I can count since the launch of *Don't Feed the Elephants! Overcoming the Art of Avoidance to Build Powerful Partnerships*. While the focus of the book was the workplace, the truth is relationships are relationships regardless of where and why they exist. The challenges, the needs, the regrettable events, the curiosity, and the courage may look different depending on the situation, but the foundation remains the same.

Alongside my colleagues, I have heard hundreds of stories about moments of profound insights, of people building new possibilities in themselves and with others, and most inspiring of all, stories of people stepping into a new place of curiosity, candor, and compassion. We have also heard how hard this work can feel—especially at the beginning when old habits are challenged and new habits are formed. It is common to feel unsure of where to start or how to sustain these practices.

Building, sustaining, and strengthening new habits can take an incredible amount of time and intentionality, as we will explore in the next chapter. Having more intentional conversations is challenging. This work happens when the stakes and stress are high—when we feel particularly emotionally tender or charged. The one thing we know from our experience is that practice may not make things easy, but it can make it easier.

We created the *Don't Feed the Elephants! Workbook* so that you can have another space to reflect further and apply your newfound insights. As you will hear us so often say, knowing isn't the same as doing, and doing when things are easy isn't the same as doing it when they are hard. Our goal for the *Don't Feed the Elephants! Workbook* is to provide another tool that continues to support your journey and commitment to show up more powerfully for yourself and for others.

The Cost of Avoidance

When I, Sarah, set out to write *Don't Feed the Elephants! Overcoming the Art of Avoidance to Build Powerful Partnerships*, my intention was to increase awareness of the avoidance that creates elephants in the room and to offer tools for my fellow avoiders of conflict to step into conversations. I had personally experienced and observed the inefficiencies, and often the pain, that came when avoidance of conversations was the norm.

As we heard more stories and observed avoidance in action, we saw even more clearly how damaging a culture of avoidance can be to individuals, relationships, and cultures. In many cases, a culture of avoidance was as damaging as a culture of aggression, sometimes even more so.

This work is critical not only for us to speak and stand with courage but to create environments where everyone can do the same.

Who Should Use This Workbook?

This workbook is intentionally designed for anyone who is interested in freeing the elephants in their world, personally or professionally. We have intentionally kept the reflections and applications general so they can be applied to the situations that will be most beneficial to you. Whether you're a partner, a parent, a sibling, a leader, a team member, a volunteer, or a human who wants to improve the quality of conversations, this workbook is for you. This workbook will help you increase your self-awareness, explore possibilities, and take intentional action.

We also want to acknowledge that while this work is informed by internal and external research, it is also informed by our worldview, which is shaped by our lived experiences, our cultural backgrounds, work experiences, and identities. Both Teresa and I are white women who grew up in the Midwest, albeit with different experiences, who now work mostly with corporate clients in the United States. Some of you might feel like how we present this work speaks to you more directly, and others may not. We are still (and will always be) evolving how we approach racial equity, privilege, and power in our work. Anytime we are talking about strategies at work, in relationships, and in groups of humans, we must consider and name the role that power, equity, and privilege play.

If you want to explore different perspectives, we'd love to recommend the following authors who have inspired our continued growth:

- Farah Harris, Author *The Color of Emotional Intelligence*
- Minda Harts, Author *Right Within and The Memo*
- Tara Jaye Frank, Author *The Waymakers*
- Elaine Lin Hering, Author *Unlearning Silence*

The most common question we get is, "Can you give me words to use?" Yes, we can provide you with words that have proven effective for us and are often recommended by experts. However, we want to qualify our suggestions. Language is subjective. The same words and tone that one person loves another will hate. When in conversation, what works for the people in it matters more than what we write on a page. Every relationship is different, just like every conversation is different. We know that some of you want something to start with, so we have provided it. Try it on; see if it fits you and your conversation. It might not work in one and might work in another.

What's Included?

The *Don't Feed the Elephants! Workbook* is a direct companion to the *Don't Feed the Elephants! Overcoming the Art of Avoidance to Build Powerful Partnerships* text. To deepen learning, more opportunities to orbit around ideas and practices helps. In fact, each time we review, summarize, reflect, and apply key ideas, we can strengthen our understanding and increase our habit building. We call this Orbital Learning.

If some of these practices and ideas are new to you, we provide a summary at the start of each chapter before examining key reflections and applications. For those of you who are familiar with this work, continue to practice your curiosity to find new connections and identify new questions.

Onward

Stepping into our curiosity, candor, and compassion can be an act of courage for many. Showing up differently in our conversations can feel uncomfortable, and that is usually where our opportunity for growth lies. As you continue your journey, be sure to give yourself grace. Each moment you engage in this work is an opportunity to make progress, a bumpy road of adventure. Just because you hit a bump doesn't mean you're going down the wrong road. Every relationship requires purposeful and ongoing calibration, and sometimes things go poorly just because someone's tired, hungry, or hurt. We hope the concepts and practices in this workbook give you fresh tools and perspectives as you continue to enhance your conversations—and ultimately your relationships—with those around you.

Sarah Noll Wilson and Dr. Teresa Peterson

How to Use This Workbook

Earlier we said that knowing is not the same as doing and that doing something when it's easy is not the same as doing it when it's challenging. Often, we confuse exposure to a topic with really understanding it and being able to do it independently when the stakes are high. One of the most common learning traps we see in our work with individuals and teams is the idea that learning is as simple as "one and done."

Here are a few of the learning traps we see frequently. Be on the lookout for these whispering in your ear as you use the workbook:

- **Overestimating what you already know**—Often sounds like, "I know this already, move on."

- **Confusing knowing for doing**—Often sounds like, "I know this already, so I must be doing this already." An added component of this is confusing the ability to do these practices when you're in an easy or safe environment with doing it when the heat is turned up and the stakes are high.

- **Believing you should get it right the first time**—Often sounds like, "I tried it and it didn't work. So I must not be good at it." People who are high achieving often fall into this trap. Watch out for the roots of perfectionism that will get in the way of your learning

- **Believing you will never get it right, so you don't try**—Often sounds like, "I will mess it up, so I won't even try." People who want to know absolutely everything about an idea before they try it on or people who don't feel they have the time to practice often fall into this trap. Again, perfectionism is usually at play behind the scenes and will sabotage learning.

The Model of Perpetual Learning

Instead of thinking of learning as a quick, transactional experience, we want you to consider the Model of Perpetual Learning as a way of building habits and supporting long-term behavior change. As you move through this workbook, we invite you to jump into the opportunity to explore, experiment, and evolve.

The goal of the **Explore** phase is to increase self-awareness and deepen your understanding of both content and behavioral patterns. Throughout this phase, you will reflect on how new information or understanding combines or collides with what you already know. You will also discover things you want to learn more about or do differently. The Explore phase might also validate something you already believe and deepen it.

While in the **Experiment** phase, your goal is to try new things. The most common thinking trap for Experiment happens when people think they need to create a robust, scientific plan. We encourage you to think of the experimentation phase as one simple question: What will I try? Try one thing differently and examine the impact. Share your experiments with a trusted colleague or friend. Share them with someone you don't know well or someone with a different life experience or perspective. You can even record them in a journal.

The final phase is **Evolve**. We take inspiration from evolution in nature to drive this process: What do we hold on to? What do we let go of? What do we create that is new or different? Focused reflection is an essential element of creating lasting learning. In our work, we find that reflection is often sacrificed in the name of "efficiency." Any time you gain in the short term by eliminating reflection will undercut your growth in the long term. Take the time to reflect.

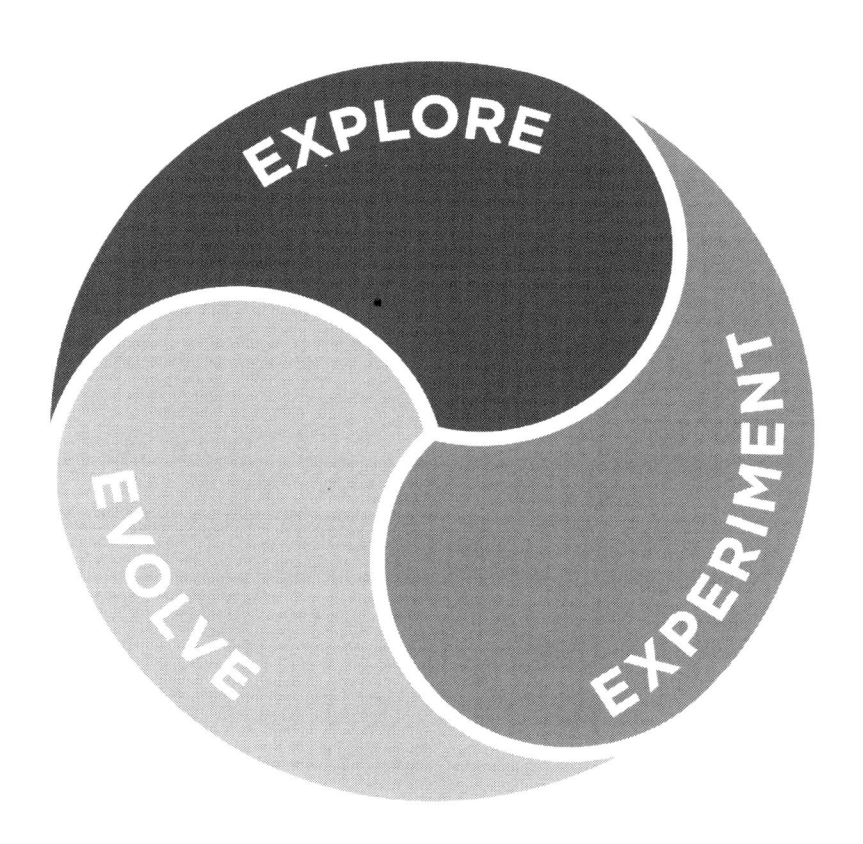

About Autopilot

Habits are easy because you don't have to think about them; they've worked for you for a long time. They're part of your autopilot. When we have conversations, we're running on habitual assumptions. As you work through this book and experiment with new practices, you will be actively pushing against your autopilot. Changing these lifelong habits requires you to reprogram your autopilot. This work requires a lot of energy and can only be performed by your executive brain. Give yourself permission to let go of being right and to be okay with getting tired, taking breaks, and trying again.

Chapter 1

Signs There Might Be an Elephant in the Room

An elephant in the room is an unaddressed conflict. We feed the elephant when we recognize it but don't address it.

The *Elephant in the Room* is not a person. The elephant is a conflict that creates a harmful barrier and goes unaddressed. If someone does something that causes an issue and there is a conversation, the conflict exists but isn't an elephant. Elephants grow when we "feed" them with our avoidant behaviors and allow them to continue to linger as opposed to addressing them.

Psychological safety represents the ability to take risks without fear of retaliation.

One crucial element in addressing an elephant is psychological safety. A common misunderstanding is that psychological safety means comfort, but safety and comfort are not the same thing. Safety is the opposite of harm. In its most basic form, psychological safety means we can talk about things that might be challenging, we can ask questions, we can learn from each other, we can take risks, and we can disagree without fearing retaliation.

If you see avoidant behaviors, you might have an elephant in the room.

To spot avoidance in the world, you can be on the lookout for these classic behaviors:

- People become quiet, shift in their seats, fidget, or change the subject
- No one responds to questions or minimal responses are given
- Dialogue is sarcastic or passive aggressive
- Body language changes—often arms are crossed, or people sit as far back as possible
- People become immersed in their phones—"urgent" calls must be taken, "urgent" emails must be replied to, unproductive messages are sent to others who are also in the meeting

If the energy has shifted suddenly, you might have an elephant in the room.

In addition to the behaviors listed, a palpable shift in the energy occurs. This shift can take the form of extremely low energy as people seek to withdraw from the conversation, or it can take an edgy, anxious kind of energy as people become increasingly uncomfortable. The most common words we hear to describe the feeling of having an elephant in the room are tense, anxious, and awkward.

It usually takes more work to avoid an elephant than to address it.

Tolerating elephants is incredibly costly. We routinely hear estimates that people spend twenty or more hours actively avoiding conversations. Recently, we had a conversation with a leader who described the cost of maintaining an elephant on a team within her organization. The team had grown from eight people to 22—not because the workload required it, but because the elephants had grown so large that they merely hired more people so the work could be done while the avoidance of one another and key issues continued.

Trust is key in not only freeing elephants, but in proactively preventing them.

It is human nature to judge ourselves by our good intentions and others by the impact they make. In terms of building trust with others, good intentions don't take us very far. Ultimately, it is our behavior on a daily basis that others use to decide if we are trustworthy. You don't get to decide if you're trustworthy. Other people do.

Explore

1. Think about a specific situation where there was an obvious issue or topic that everyone avoided discussing. What made it difficult to address?

___

___

___

___

___

2. In your experience, how does the elephant in the room affect the dynamics of a conversation or relationship?

_____

_____

_____

_____

3. What emotions arise for you when you're aware of an elephant in the room? How do you typically respond?

_____

_____

_____

_____

4. Reflect on a time when you chose to ignore an elephant in the room. What were the consequences of that choice?

_____

_____

_____

_____

5. In what ways have your past experiences with conflict, communication, and collaboration shaped your current approach to addressing uncomfortable topics?

6. How do you typically respond when someone else addresses the elephant in the room?

7. Reflect on a time when someone successfully freed an elephant in the room. What factors internally and externally contributed to that success?

8. When you think of where you are currently in your comfort and skill with addressing elephants in your world, what do you want to hold onto? What would you like to do new or differently?

_____

_____

_____

_____

_____

_____

_____

Experiment

Courageous Audit: Uncovering Your Avoidant Behaviors

Although there are many similarities in how we show avoidance, everyone has their own internal and external "tells." Identifying your tells is a meaningful step in the journey of overcoming avoidance. Watch out for shame and guilt—they love to show up during Courageous Audits.

1. How do you know when you are avoiding?

_____

_____

_____

_____

_____

_____

2. How do you know when you are in the balance of choosing avoidance over having a conversation?

3. What sensations do you feel in your body?

4. What thoughts go through your mind?

5. Where do you look? How do you sit?

6. What facial expressions do you make?

7. What do you do with your hands and feet?

8. Where do you feel tension in your body?

___

Now that you have conducted a Courageous Audit of your avoidant behaviors, be on the lookout for them. When you feel a sensation, feel your eyebrow raise, or start tapping your pencil, get curious with yourself. Notice and name these behaviors. You're likely to discover more about yourself and your relationship with conflict and avoidance now that you're paying attention.

Bonus Points: Share your new insights about yourself with a trusted friend or colleague.

Chapter 2

This Is What Your Brain Is Doing on Stress

Because our brain's primary function is keeping us alive, it constantly scans for threats.

Much of our brain function is unconscious to us. Our breathing, heartbeat, and digestion happen without conscious thought. Our amygdala also works under our radar to keep us alive by constantly scanning for threats. These threats can be physical or emotional; they might be right in front of us, or they might be imagined. Adults often have a negative reaction to the word "imagined" because it can sound illogical, so you could also think of it as an anticipated threat—something within the realm of possibility.

When our amygdala perceives a threat, it sends hormones into our system to allow us to act. While these hormones are invaluable in some situations, they are usually quite inconvenient in a conversation. When the amygdala takes over, the cortisol and adrenaline in our system shuts down access to the higher functioning parts of our brains to focus on survival. When our brain is in this flooded state, we are not able to explore perspectives, consider meaningful solutions, or build connections with others. A brain under stress is an untrusting brain. We are more likely to have a stress response when we are tired, hungry, hurt, or when things are uncertain or unpredictable.

All humans experience stress responses.

There are five major stress responses. All of these are normal and natural, and we experience all of them at some point in our lives. There is no "good" or "bad" stress response, but some of the behaviors that accompany them can be unproductive in certain situations. We are usually quick to forgive ourselves for our stress responses, but not to give others the same grace. We have stress responses because we are human.

STRESS RESPONSE	PRODUCTIVE BEHAVIORS	UNPRODUCTIVE BEHAVIORS
FIGHT- Inspires defensive or aggressive action 	Setting boundaries; advocating for yourself or others; establishing a non-negotiable	Aggressive words or actions, blaming, controlling, physical violence
FLIGHT- Inspires a desire to escape 	Removing yourself from a harmful situation; knowing when you need a break	Complete avoidance or unwillingness to have a conversation or interaction
FREEZE- Inspires us to stop immediately 	Pausing to assess a situation; delaying action until a more appropriate time	Ruminating or prolonged mental paralysis—overly analyzing, perfectionism
FAWN- Inspires us to eliminate the stress for others for our own safety and sometimes at our own expense 	Listening; compromising; looking for a win-win	Giving up your own needs or compromising your boundary for the other person's benefit; agreeing to something or acting in a way you know is wrong
FLOCK- Inspires us to make meaning with others 	Processing an event; seeking validation, perspectives, or coaching	Only surrounding yourself with those who agree with you; talking about a person, but never with them; continued focus on negative experiences or situations

In our work with individuals and teams, we see three distinct trends regarding stress responses:

1. Most people will publicly identify *fight* as their default, so if you do too, you're not alone. We suspect this is partially due to *fight* being a socially acceptable response in many cultures, especially for men.

2. *Flocking* is probably the least understood and most underestimated stress response. Our default is often to view people talking together as "cliques," "meetings after the meetings," "stirring up drama," or simply "plotting." But it is one of the first places our brain will go under stress.

3. Most people report having a different default response at home compared to at work or with friends.

Because our brain's primary job is to keep us alive, it easily accepts information about things that might be harmful. One way our brain does that is to focus on negative inputs and experiences and transfer them into our long-term memories. This is also why we assume a group of people *flocking* is up to no good. Necessary from a survival perspective? Yes. Extremely frustrating almost all the time? Also, yes. Because our brain is wired to more readily accept negative information—and fill in any unknown information with negative predictions—we must make time to actively seek other perspectives, consider other interpretations, and reflect objectively.

Explore

1. Which stress responses do you think you have most often?

_____

_____

_____

_____

2. Think about situations at work, at home, or in other settings like a sports team, club, or volunteer work. How do your stress responses vary by your role or location? What about when working with people you lead compared to your response with your leader?

3. What messages did you receive growing up about stress responses and ways it was appropriate to react to stress (or not react)? What about in your professional life? How might these messages play a role in the way you respond to stress now?

4. When our amygdala triggers, it takes around 18 minutes for the stress hormones to fully peak and then 24 hours to fully recover. Knowing this, what strategies can you use to support yourself in the moment and throughout the next day to regulate and recover?

5. What contributes to your stress response venturing into the unhealthy or unproductive zone?

6. Are there specific interventions you can think of that help you move from an unhealthy place to a healthy one?

7. What new strategies might you try, and when would be a good opportunity to try them?

Experiment

Conduct an Amygdala Audit

Our amygdala's job is to protect us from threats to our physical or emotional safety.

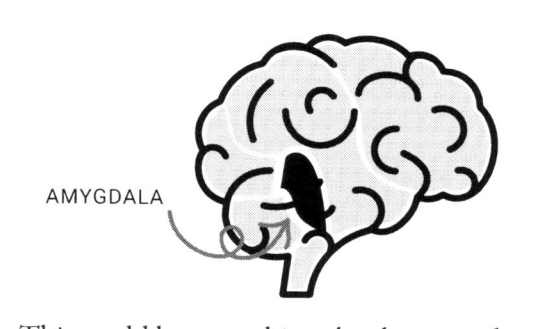

1. Think about a time when you had a stress response. This could be something that happened either in or out of work.

2. Reflect—What does it feel like when your amygdala is triggered? Think about the reactions you feel in both your body and your mind.

3. Are there patterns in the types of situations or interactions that trigger your amygdala?

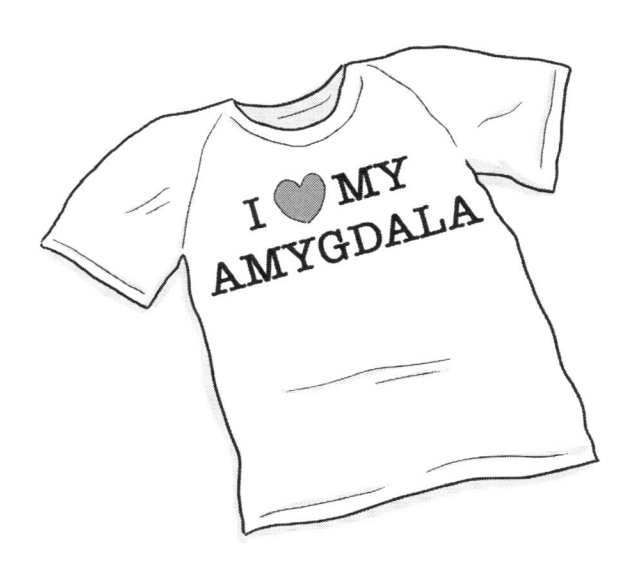

___

Chapter 3

Naming Your Elephants

Elephants are created by avoidance.

Sometimes we avoid to maintain our comfort. We may avoid because of previous experiences or trauma. We may avoid because the risk of having the conversation feels too high. We may avoid because we don't have the tools to have the conversation. We may avoid to protect our power, position, and privilege. We may avoid because we are tired and don't have the energy. While we use the word avoid to define the behavior, we have to understand that avoiding conflict doesn't mean it disappears. Our friend and colleague T. Maxine Woods-McMillan Esq. powerfully says, "You don't avoid conflict; you just displace or reposition it." Are you ready to go elephant spotting?

Elephant Spotting Guide

The different types of elephants we list are meant to be helpful and fun, but they aren't meant to be overwhelming, dismissive, to stall progress, or to be a barrier to action. We invite you to explore the different types but not to worry too much about a diagnosis of the elephant(s) you're facing. The good news is that the steps forward are the same.

How Does it Feel When an Elephant is in the Room?

TENSE—The language around tension can include the following: "A fog that is tight around the chest, shoulders tight, sick to the stomach, nervous through the whole meeting."

ANXIOUS—You may feel heavy and anxious. There may be discomfort from feelings of uncertainty about how people will respond or what will happen afterward.

FEARFUL—You might have questions like, "Will I be shunned for speaking up? Will there be retaliation? Will I hurt someone? Will I be hurt if we can't talk about it?"

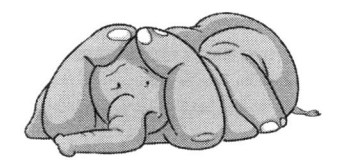

The Avoidephant
(a·void'·eh·fent)

When we avoid action to remove the internal stress of a situation, an "Avoidephant" is created.

Avoidephants are our archetype—the basis from which all the future elephant species we'll discuss in this book have derived. An Avoidephant pushes itself in the way of anyone trying to initiate a necessary conversation and keeps team members from clarifying important information.

In the presence of an Avoidephant, we literally avoid conversations, opting to internalize our thoughts, feelings, and insights.

"I know they're a good person, but..." • "It's not that big of a deal anyway..." • "I didn't want them to feel bad..."

The Imagiphant
(ee·maj'·eh·fent)

The act of holding frustration without an effort to clarify is what summons the "Imagiphant."

The Imagiphant species of Avoidephants are born from stories you've told yourself and assumptions you've made without confirming or testing your beliefs.

Although the feelings you're having may not be based on the truth, it doesn't make it less real for you because it's your truth. When you lock yourself into one perspective about a situation or person without taking the time to consider other possibilities, a hungry little Imagiphant grows and grows.

"No, I know that's not what they meant." • "Oh, that's just how they are." • "I don't need to ask. I just know."

The Blamephant
(blame'·eh·fent)

When we complain instead of acting on problems, there's a good chance we have a "Blamephant" in the room.

One of the most common ways to feed a Blamephant—another pesky species of Avoidephant—in a team is to blame someone else or the situation instead of reflecting.

At some point, we've all been in a situation where we know there's a barrier, and instead of acting, we blame other people's action or inaction for that barrier.

"Can you believe they did that?!" • "It's not what I'd do, but..." • "I don't know why they'd make that decision!"

The Nudgephant
(nuj´·eh·fent)

We feed a "Nudgephant" when we see a barrier, and instead of addressing the issue directly, we try to nudge our team forward with indirect effort.

We sugarcoat our words or drop hints instead of making statements. When we're dealing with a Nudgephant, it means we've worked up a little bit of courage to approach an issue, but it might not be enough.

If you and your team are dancing around an issue without diving in to address it, you may have a Nudgephant in the room. Sometimes a nudge is what is needed to get the conversation going; when you nudge and there is no movement, then you have a Nudgephant.

"I tried to have the conversation, but..." • "Maybe we could..." • "Do you think it might make sense to..."

The Deflectephant
(dah·fleck´·ta·fent)

A "Deflectephant" gets a handful of peanuts whenever someone makes a joke, displays sarcastic or self-deprecating behavior, or attempts to create a detour in response to an uncomfortable situation.

When a situation gets uncomfortable, the Deflectephant likes to whisper in the ear of the office jokester or quickly shift topics.

The Deflectephant aids diversion. When someone is unwilling to be vulnerable, they may attempt to minimize or hide their own discomfort by creating discomfort in other people or creating a distraction.

"Let's agree to disagree." • "It was just a joke! You're too sensitive." • "I don't think this is that big of a deal."

Explore

1. Which types of elephants feel most familiar to you?

_____

_____

_____

_____

_____

2. Is there a particular type that is most common in your workplace? In your family? What conditions and specific behaviors allow those elephants to develop?

3. Which elephants do you feel most comfortable tolerating?

4. Which elephants are you most sensitive to or irritated by? What insights do you have about that?

5. Think about an elephant currently taking up space in your life. How did it begin? What might be possible if it were freed?

_____

_____

_____

_____

_____

_____

_____

_____

We have heard from many others who have identified new elephant types as they have examined their behaviors. Here are a few new species we've discovered:

Perfectaphant—When we won't have the conversation unless everything is just perfect (which means we never have the conversation).

Pretendaphant—When everyone pretends that something that was said or done just didn't happen and continues to go on without acknowledging it.

Optimaphant—When you lean into your optimistic belief that everything will work out without taking any action to help it work out.

Gaslightaphant—When someone convinces you that what you saw or experienced didn't happen in order to avoid acknowledging or addressing.

Grenadephant—When someone throws an emotional or mental grenade into a situation and immediately leaves.

What new elephant species would you add that you have created or observed others create?

Elephant Type 1: _____

What behaviors does this elephant thrive on? _____

_____

_____

_____

_____

_____

_____

What do you see and hear when this elephant is present? _____

_____

_____

_____

_____

_____

_____

Elephant Type 2: _____

What behaviors does this elephant thrive on? _____

_____

_____

_____

_____

_____

_____

What do you see and hear when this elephant is present? _____

_____

_____

_____

_____

_____

_____

Elephant Type 3: _____

What behaviors does this elephant thrive on? _____

_____

_____

_____

_____

_____

_____

What do you see and hear when this elephant is present? _____

_____

_____

_____

_____

_____

_____

Please share your new elephant types with us! Send us the name and description to: **hello@sarahnollwilson.com**, and we may use it in future work!

Experiment

Part of the work of moving from avoidance to action is building up our awareness. Over the next week, see if you can notice and name an elephant that you created or are feeding. Depending on the quality of the relationship and the trust with the people in your world, challenge yourself to name it out loud by saying something like, "I realize I've been feeding an Avoidaphant." Or if they aren't familiar with this language you might try, "I realize I've been avoiding talking to you about X."

Please note that the intention behind the lighthearted names for elephants is to help us see our behaviors with greater nuance and reduce some of the stress that may come along with acknowledging our avoidance. The goal is not perfection with language or naming conventions. You might not even use these terms in your conversations, but rather use them as an internal tool of reflection.

1. What elephant are you or were you feeding?

___

2. How were you avoiding the conversation? What were your avoidant behaviors?

3. How did it feel to name it out loud?

4. If you shared your insights with another person, how did they respond?

5. What is possible for you and this situation by naming your avoidance, even if you just name it internally?

Chapter 4

Are You Feeding the Elephant?

When it comes to conversations, we most often hear that people want to speak honestly and directly without causing harm or discomfort. That does sound wonderful, doesn't it? In fact, nine out of 10 conversations miss the mark according to Judith E. Glaser and her work on Conversational Intelligence. Sometimes we aren't clear enough. Sometimes we are distracted or on autopilot. Sometimes we don't check for understanding between the speaker and the listener. Sometimes we want to provoke or attack. And... sometimes...we feed an elephant to avoid the conversation entirely.

We feed elephants because avoiding usually feels more comfortable than addressing them...in the short term anyway.

Why do we feed elephants?

Here are a few common reasons people might decide to not have a conversation. Take a moment and read through the different examples. Consider which ones resonate with you, which ones might feel uncomfortable to consider, and which ones you have not experienced but someone else might have experienced.

- **Fear of Consequences:** Many people avoid tough conversations because they fear potential fallout. Questions like, "Will I be excluded?", "Will this harm my career?", "Will I damage important relationships?" are common. People worry about what might happen if they speak up—will they lose relationships, opportunities, or even respect? For example, an employee might hesitate to bring up a recurring issue in meetings because they fear being seen as a complainer, which could damage their reputation or career prospects. Similarly, a middle manager might avoid raising concerns about unrealistic deadlines because they don't want to risk straining relationships with upper management.

- **Fear of Loss:** It's not really change people fear—it's what they might lose in the process. Someone might hold back from bringing up issues because they're scared of losing status, comfort, or a sense of safety. For example, an LGBTQ+ employee might avoid talking about discriminatory practices because they fear losing their sense of belonging in the team, even if it might lead to positive changes. Or a long-tenured employee might resist new systems because they're worried about losing the familiarity and expertise that give them value in their role.

- **Desire to Protect Power:** Those with power might steer clear of tough conversations to hold onto their power or influence. Maybe a white manager avoids addressing racial biases because they're afraid it could make them look vulnerable or jeopardize their authority. Or a senior employee might ignore team conflicts to maintain their image as a neutral leader, even if it means allowing problems to fester.

- **Systemic Silencing and Retaliation:** For some, speaking up feels risky because they've seen what happens when others do—it doesn't end well. Women of color, for example, often get sidelined or punished for raising concerns about discrimination or inequity. Individuals in lower-power positions, like an entry-level worker, may stay quiet about mistreatment because they fear being labeled as difficult or even losing their job. The fear of systemic retaliation can prevent anyone—regardless of background—from addressing issues that challenge entrenched power structures.

- **Normalization of Harmful Behavior:** Sometimes, harmful behavior becomes so routine that no one even questions it anymore. In a high-pressure workplace, for example, constant overwork might be the norm, so people avoid bringing up work-life balance issues because it's just "how things are done."

- **Emotional and Cognitive Overload:** Tackling tough issues takes energy that some people just don't have. A parent juggling work and home life might choose to ignore unrealistic deadlines at work because they don't have the mental space to fight that battle. Or someone facing microaggressions might decide it's not worth the exhaustion of explaining their experience yet again, especially if they've been brushed off in the past.

- **Perception of Futility or Hopelessness:** When people believe that speaking up won't lead to meaningful change, they may decide it's not worth the effort. For instance, a long-serving employee who has seen past attempts to change company culture go nowhere might stop voicing concerns, believing that their input won't make a difference. Similarly, someone from a marginalized group may have experienced being dismissed or ignored when raising issues about bias, leading them to feel that speaking up won't change anything.

- **Internalized Beliefs and Biases:** Sometimes the barriers are within. Internalized beliefs can lead people to doubt whether their concerns are worth raising. Someone struggling with mental health issues might avoid bringing them up at work because they've internalized the stigma that says they should just "tough it out."

How do we feed elephants?

There are dozens of elephant-feeding behaviors—both that we've done ourselves and we've heard from others. Here are a few responses:

- We avoid asking for what we need. When we don't share our needs, boundaries, or expectations, the conditions are just right for frustration to build and barriers to begin.

- We might talk to everyone except the person we should be talking to about an issue. We might blame, criticize, or plot. We might deflect or minimize an issue on our teams because they haven't personally affected us yet or because we want to appear to be "above" conflict. Sometimes we want to maintain the façade that our team has no conflict at all. (PS, when people tell us their team has no conflict, it's a big red flag for us.)

- We hold untested assumptions. Our assumptions were likely true at one time but might not be true now. We often allow our assumptions to fill in the rest of a story or to justify our lack of action.

- We defer to someone else—usually the formal leader or HR. Typically under the guise of "not stepping on someone's toes," we likely defer as a form of work avoidance and to maintain personal comfort.

Before you complete the Courageous Audit and behavior inventory that follow, let's make sure that three ideas are firmly at the front of our minds.

Be on the lookout for the **Shame, Shame, Boomerang**. When we closely examine our own behaviors, it is normal to have a variety of feelings and reactions. We might feel disappointed in ourselves or frustrated by old habits that are hard to break. Once we feel shame, we often shame ourselves for feeling shame to begin with... and here comes the Shame, Shame, Boomerang. While we are big believers in allowing ourselves to feel all our emotions, shame is an incredibly destructive one. Not only does shame feel terrible, but it will also undercut your attempts at behavior change. Shame keeps you stuck in the past instead of looking at the possibility of the future.

Instead of letting yourself get beat up repeatedly by the Shame, Shame, Boomerang, you might try to **Celebrate the Catch**.

As you move through the rest of this chapter, you'll likely find behaviors that you would like to change. You can discover things you want to start doing as well as things you want to stop doing. Once you focus on changing your behavior, it's very common to notice the unwanted behavior or thought after it's passed. We see it like a mile marker on the interstate that we drive by quickly. When you notice that you've passed the mile marker—that is, doing the very thing you didn't want to do anymore—Celebrate the Catch. Congratulations—you're switching your behavior off autopilot, and that takes a lot of work! As we continue Celebrating the Catch, our minds become more consciously aware of our behavior. Just like when we slow down our car, we can see the mile markers more clearly, our brain can slow down to see our default behavior before it happens. Once we've reached the point of proactively seeing our behavior, we can change it. Keep Celebrating the Catch as you go—the brain is highly motivated by the hit of dopamine that happens when we do a great job.

Finally, while this is a workbook to help you have the conversations you are avoiding, we don't think that's always the best option. It is important to note that in some situations, consciously avoiding is perfectly viable and sometimes necessary. Perhaps this isn't a battle that you want to fight. Maybe you don't have the emotional bandwidth right now. Maybe it really will be dangerous.

The goal of the activities that follow is to help you identify how and why you avoid. The goal is not to persuade you to attempt to free an elephant in every situation.

Explore

Reflection—Elephant Feeding

We have all fed elephants. You might even have a peanut in your hand right now! Let's take a courageous look at our own elephant feeding patterns.

1. Consider a time in the past when you fed an elephant in your professional life—that is you chose avoidance over purposeful action or conversation. What was the situation? What about it felt risky? What might have been at stake? Why did avoidance feel like the right choice at the time? How did the situation resolve?

   _____
   _____
   _____
   _____
   _____
   _____
   _____

2. Consider a time in your personal life that you have fed an elephant. What was the situation? What about it felt risky? What might have been at stake? Why did avoidance feel justified? What resolution, if any, has occurred?

   _____
   _____
   _____
   _____
   _____
   _____

3. Think about an elephant you're currently feeding. What is the situation? Who is involved? What about it feels risky or uncertain? What might be at stake? Why might avoidance not be the best choice? What might be possible if the situation could be resolved? What resolution would you like to see?

_____
_____
_____
_____
_____
_____
_____
_____
_____

4. What patterns do you see in your reflections on the questions above? What insights have you gained about yourself? What are you curious about when you think about avoidance? What are you curious about when you think about freeing elephants?

_____
_____
_____
_____
_____
_____
_____

Experiment

Courageous Audit—Ways I Have Fed Elephants

A Courageous Audit requires us to put our own behavior under a microscope. It takes courage to see the ways we contribute to problems or to recognize when we behave in ways that are contrary to our desired impact. PS. During a Courageous Audit, it's very normal to let out a big sigh or feel a little uncomfortable at some point.

How have you fed an elephant? What behaviors have kept a conflict alive or maintained your avoidance of the real issue?

A very short list of ways we've fed elephants:

- Changed the subject when it got too close to the real issue
- Sugarcoated the truth or reality
- Talked to the wrong people/Talked to everyone except the person involved
- Said "it's fine" when it wasn't fine
- Minimized the severity of a situation
- Made assumptions about the other person to justify the decision to continue avoiding
- Decided not to "push a topic" because we believed we were the only one it impacted or the only one who cared
- Made assumptions about the other person to justify my decision to continue avoiding

Fill in the peanuts below with the specific behaviors you have done to feed an elephant.

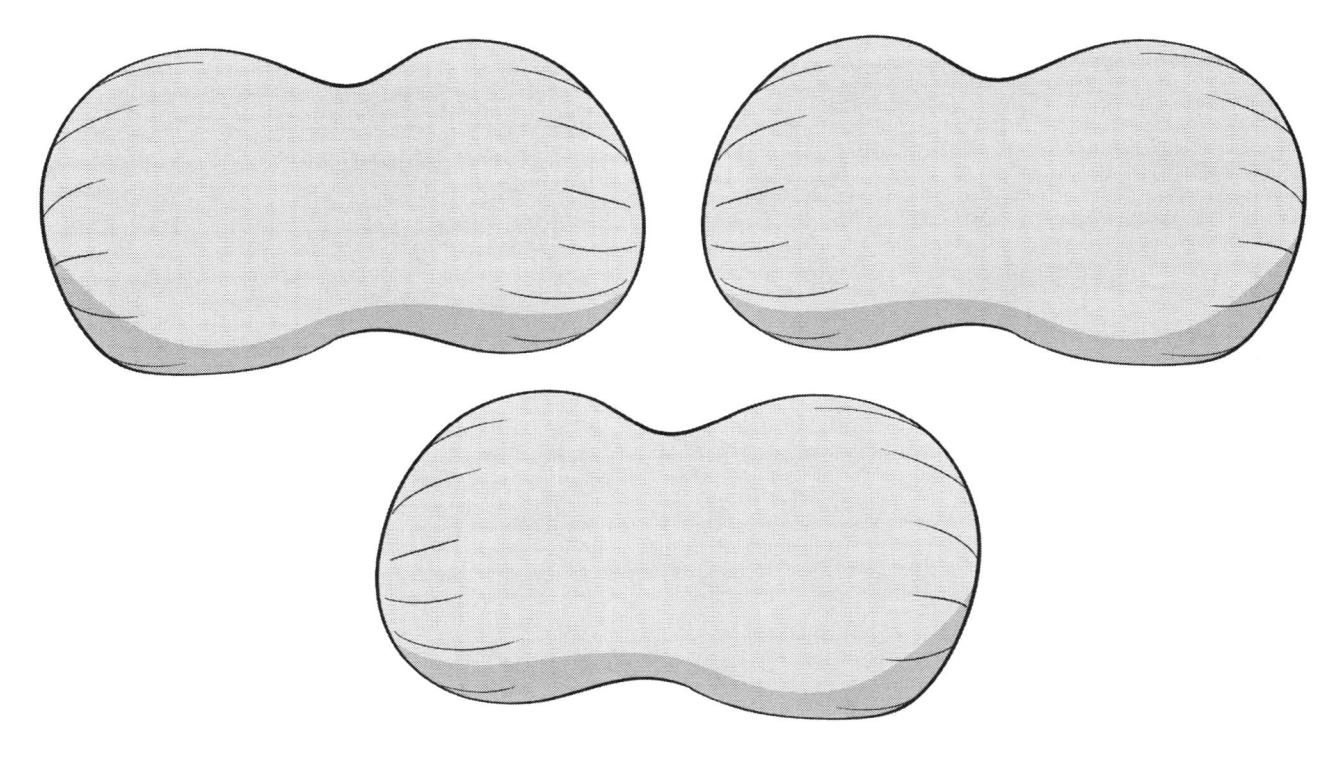

Chapter 5

Step One: Be Curious with Yourself

If your first reaction to the very thought of discussing an elephant is avoidance, you are certainly not alone. What we gain in the short term by avoiding doesn't usually pay off in the long term. For many of us, we are considering what we stand to lose. Loss aversion focuses us on the downside to such an extent that the potential gain has to be significantly greater to make it feel worthwhile. Since our brain's primary function is keeping us safe, it can overestimate risks to prevent us from doing something that feels uncertain. Fortunately, freeing elephants is usually easier (not necessarily easy) and more manageable than most people imagine. It all starts with curiosity.

Curiosity opens our mind and our heart.

Why curiosity? Simply put, curiosity primes our brain for learning and engages the most sophisticated parts of our brain. Unlike the tunnel vision that results in an amygdala hijack, where the brain is focused solely on survival, curiosity creates a beautiful display of synaptic fireworks in the brain, which allows us to focus on exploration, connection, learning, and possibility.

In our work with thousands of leaders every year, we find that curiosity is one factor that the very best leaders exhibit regularly. They model curiosity themselves, and they foster and reward it in others. They know how to sit with the potential discomfort of not knowing the answer immediately. They know there are often multiple answers to questions.

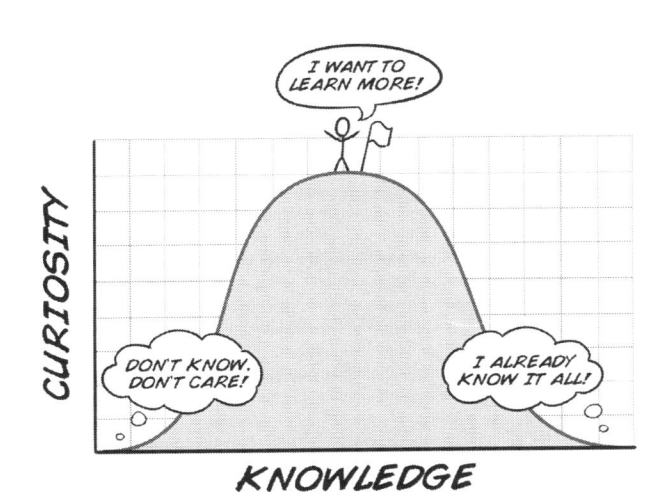

There is a sweet spot for curiosity, and it's located where we know enough to want to know more.

Recently, someone in a session said, "Curiosity? Sure, I do that all the time. I pretend not to know the answer. Sometimes I just play stupid and then ask questions so they can get to my answer." To be clear, this isn't curiosity. Curiosity is a genuine desire to know more about someone or something and a belief that there are always things you don't know. Here are a few other examples to make sure we're all on the same page.

It's not curiosity if...

- You already know the answer
- You already have a position, and your only goal is guiding someone else to your position
- You are pretending not to know
- You don't want to know the answer or don't really care
- You are only looking to validate your own idea

The Curiosity First Approach™ to conversations has three specific practices.

The tools in this section will focus on the first step in the process—getting curious with yourself. Why start with yourself? We have observed over the many years of doing this work that when people are struggling with a situation or person, they stop at the feelings of frustration and don't examine or define what is causing the frustration. Specific to relationships, when there is an issue, usually it is because there is a need that isn't being met or a value of ours that is being stepped on or not honored. By getting clarity on our own perspectives, we might realize we don't need to have a conversation or we might be primed for a more productive conversation.

Taking time to get curious with yourself is often the most challenging step of the whole process. It is often our tendency to look outward, to assume, and to point our fingers.

- Be curious with yourself
- Be curious about the other person
- Be curious with the other person

Explore

Tool—Reflection: Curiosity

One of the best ways to begin getting curious is to reflect on your relationship with curiosity itself. Ask yourself the following questions:

1. In which roles in my life (leader, team member, parent, sibling, friend, child, coach, volunteer) does curiosity come most easily? In which roles is it most challenging? What insights do you have about the differences?

2. In what situations or under what conditions is it easiest to be curious? In what situations or conditions is it difficult to lean into curiosity?

3. When does curiosity feel like a risk?

4. What assumptions do you hold about curiosity? What stories do you tell yourself about curiosity?

5. Think about a time you were able to utilize curiosity in a conversation. What behaviors or mindsets were involved? How do you think curiosity affected the outcome?

Experiment

Practice—Get Curious with Yourself

When you find yourself in a conflict, the first step toward resolving it is getting curious with yourself. Beginning with a focus on yourself helps clarify your perspective and your needs. It helps you focus on the heart of the issue as opposed to the small annoyances that might be wrapped up with it.

Take a moment and think about a current situation you are struggling with or a challenge you anticipate facing. Consider some of the questions that follow. You don't need to answer all of these questions every time you are thinking about a conflict or preparing for a conversation. Also know this isn't an exhaustive list. You may come up with additional questions that would be helpful to explore, and we encourage you to do so.

1. What am I feeling? (Hint: If it's anger, keep digging. Anger is a secondary emotion, which means we feel it after we've felt something else first. The first feeling might be something like fear, disappointment, or shame.)

2. What is important to me?

3. What is my perspective?

4. What do I need? What need is not being met?

5. What do I know to be true? (This can be a great question when there might be an Imagiphant involved.)

_____

_____

_____

_____

_____

6. What might I be missing?

_____

_____

_____

_____

_____

7. Is this a preference or a performance issue?

_____

_____

_____

_____

_____

8. What assumptions am I making?

9. What role have I played or am I playing in this situation?

Reflection

1. What has become clearer about this conflict as a result of getting curious with yourself?

2. What might be the benefits of doing this more frequently?

3. What questions would you add to this list?

___

___

___

___

___

___

___

PS. The most common concern we hear about this process is time commitment, but we have found that you can gain a lot of clarity in just a few minutes of focused reflection utilizing these questions. Also, you likely don't need to reflect on everything you're doing. Choose one or two instances where you think a change could help in future interactions.

Chapter 6

Step Two: Be Curious About Others

While getting curious about ourselves helps us more clearly understand what makes sense to us, the second step primes us to understand what makes sense to the other person.

One way we can think about what makes sense to one another is by thinking about our differences through the concept of living on islands. Think of each person as operating from a unique island where their preferences, their lived experiences, their values, their personality, and their skills live. Your island is perfect for you. Likewise, my island is perfect for me. Additionally, we don't have the same vantage point from our individual islands, so no matter how similar we might be, we will never be the same or have the exact same perspectives.

Sometimes, after we get curious about another person, we find we haven't taken enough time to get to know them or to understand their island. Therefore, we either made up a lot about their island, assuming it was like ours (an egocentric bias) or assumed it was very different (a stereotype). In this situation, a conversation about islands and designing an island together is often a great path forward in conversation. For your reference, we've included the islands framework at the end of this chapter.

There are a few traps we can fall into when we get curious about others, so use caution.

Getting Curious About Others Isn't:	Getting Curious About Others Is:
Coming to conclusions about their perspectives or filling in their stories for them.	Considering that they have a perspective and stories that are unique and different from your own, and there's overlap.
Judging the merits of their ideas, needs, or values.	Seeking to understand their ideas, needs, and values.
Elevating their needs above your own.	Looking for the balance of both needs.

Remember, the practice of curiosity is an invitation, not a prescription. There may be times when getting curious about the other person isn't what the moment needs or what is appropriate. For example, we would never ask someone who had suffered abuse to get curious about their abuser. If someone has experienced racism in the workplace, it is generally not useful to ask, "What do you think their perspective was?" because it will be a rejection of their experience.

Explore

Practice—Get Curious About Others

Taking the time to get curious about other people helps us remember that we all come from different places and that everyone has perspectives worth considering. In a conflict, it's very easy for us to cope by othering or assuming the worst about the other parties involved. This set of questions seeks to illuminate possibility and humanize everyone involved, which makes a resolution much more likely.

Below are some questions to get you started. You don't need to answer all of these questions every time you are thinking about a conflict or preparing for a conversation. You'll notice that these questions use tentative language—using words like "might" helps us focus on a range of possible answers, not just one or two.

1. What signals and behaviors did I see that made me think they came with a certain feeling? (Hint: If it's anger, keep digging. Anger is a secondary emotion, which means they feel it after they've felt something else first. The first feeling might be something like fear, disappointment, or shame.)

_____

_____

_____

_____

2. What information or knowledge do I think they had before the conflict?

_____

_____

_____

_____

3. What do I know to be important to them and how did this situation fit or not fit in those priorities?

4. What do they value? Where are those values in this situation or conflict?

5. What things do I know that they might not know?

6. What pressures do I know they are under and how might that impact their reaction?

_____
_____
_____
_____
_____
_____

7. What do I know about how they respond to stress?

_____
_____
_____
_____
_____
_____

8. Is this a stress response I'm familiar with? If so, which one?

_____
_____
_____
_____
_____
_____

9. Do I know what helps them decrease their stress levels?

10. Do I think they trust and value me?

11. How does that affect our responses to this conflict?

12. Do I know what a caring response looks like for this person?

Reflection

1. What has become clearer about this conflict by getting curious about the others involved?

2. What might be the benefits of doing this more frequently?

3. What insight did you gain into how you might approach the situation?

Experiment

Framework—Islands

Every one of us has an island that is uniquely our own. The most powerful partnerships involve people creating a shared island where all can feel valued and thrive.

Your Island Is Perfect... For You

Our islands are made up of our preferences, skills, habits, pet peeves, lived experiences, and values. Your island makes perfect sense to you, and that's ok. The problem isn't that we have our own islands—it's that we want to force other people onto it instead of appreciating that they have their own perfect islands too.

Powerful Partnerships Create New Possibilities

When we create an island together, we navigate our shared preferences and honor non-negotiables. We find common ground where we can both have our needs met and continue to learn and evolve, which creates new possibilities. Here are the four basic steps you can take to build an island together:

1. **Think about your island.** What makes your island feel just right for you? Consider your preferences, skills, habits, pet peeves, lived experiences, and values. One common issue we find is that people haven't thought enough about their own islands, which is the first critical step in creating one with another person. Be sure you think about what is true for you and not what you think you're supposed to include.

2. **Ask others about their islands.** Listen with the intention of learning about the other person and not to make judgements or comparisons. This concept may be new for them as well, so make sure you provide them with time to process before engaging in a conversation if needed.

3. **Create your island together.** Another way we can think about this is to create collective commitments. How will we work together? How will we celebrate our work? How will we navigate the sticky situations that are going to come up? What will we do when we don't show up at our best?

4. **Islands need maintenance, so revisit them periodically.** As people continue to be shaped by new experiences, you'll need to check in about the status of your shared islands. It's very natural to have these conversations at the start of a new calendar or fiscal year, after a new team member joins or someone leaves the team, or after positions change.

Chapter 7

Step Three: Be Curious with Others

Because we are motivated to avoid having some conversations, we sometimes avoid even thinking about having the conversation. Another trend we see is that people overestimate their ability to have a successful conversation without any planning. When we use the Curiosity First Approach, by the time we're ready to get curious with the other person, we've already done most of the hard work. We have taken the time to get curious with ourselves and considered the possible perspectives of the other person involved. Bravo! It's also common that by investing the time into the first two steps you have found a potential entry point into the conversation. Hold onto it for now—we'll come back to that later.

Here are a few traps we can fall into when we get curious with others:

Instead of...	We recommend...
Preparing for a confrontation	Preparing for a conversation
Oversimplified or binary thinking	Exploring possibilities—challenging ourselves to come with at least three ideas
Only wearing your own lens; Listening for what makes sense to you	Trying to see through their lens; Listening for what makes sense to them
Expecting someone who surfaces a problem to solve it	Allowing problems to be surfaced safely by anyone; Acknowledging that one person in isolation is unlikely to be able to solve it
Focusing all your energy on one high-stakes conversation where everything must be resolved	Striving for a successful first conversation that leaves the door open for more dialogue; Tolerating non-closure in the initial conversation
Believing that raising the heat will destroy the team or that heat will melt a relationship	Embracing a mindset that effective teams have conflict and can thrive because of it; heat can forge a relationship
Wanting to be heard; escalations happen when both people want to be heard, but no one's getting through	Wanting to hear the other person

One very common thinking trap we see within teams and organizations is the belief that discussing a problem somehow creates the problem (or that the problem doesn't exist if it isn't talked about with the relevant people). On the contrary, the problem exists whether we choose to talk about it or not. Openly addressing it is the best way to remedy the problem and move forward in a stronger and more purposeful way; pretending it's not there won't help anyone. And... for what it's worth...people are probably already talking about the problem whether you know it or not.

As you begin preparing for a conversation, it's important to remember that there is no script we can give you that will lead to a magical outcome. We can, however, help you think through your mindset and your tone. We frequently hear, "Just tell me the exact words to say, and it will all be fine." When we focus only on the "right words," we lose sight of all the other things that we are experiencing and trying to manage during a conversation. Also, words that will work for one person might not work for another. There is no one "right phrase," and by focusing on the "right words," we fail to pay attention to the other factors at play. These factors can include your emotions, their emotions, expectations, the potential for retaliation or non-closure, the power dynamics at play, and the possibility of bumping into them at the grocery store. Okay, while this last one is a little tongue in cheek, it is a real concern we've heard from folks.

Reflection

Here are a few questions you might consider as you prepare for your conversation:

1. What is the goal of your conversation?

_____

_____

_____

_____

_____

_____

_____

_____

2. What is your past and/or current relationship with the person?

3. Who else may need to be part of the dialogue?

4. What elements could set the conversation up for success?

5. How will you know if your conversation is veering off track?

6. What is a good starting phrase? How do you want to start the conversation?

7. What values do you want to be true to or hold closely during the conversation?

8. What is your entry point?

9. What is the best location for talking?

10. How much time do you want to hold for this conversation?

11. What comes after the conversation? If it's going to be tough, don't send someone to an important meeting afterwards or cut the conversation short because you have something else to get to.

___

12. How do you plan to invite the person into a conversation? "HR meeting" rarely makes someone feel good if it's not common. Are you going to ask them in-person, via email, or send them a meeting request? What do you know about their workflow preferences?

___

As you prepare for the conversation, it can be helpful to think about your opening statement and extending an invitation for dialogue. We will spend more time on opening statements in the experimentation section. As a reminder, some people will like these starters and others won't. Here are a few examples:

- I know our last project faced some delays, and it felt like there was a lot of friction within our team. Would you be open to talking about it? I would like to hear how things have been from your perspective and if there's a way we can reset before the new project kicks off next week.

- During the (fill in event of your choice here—meeting, presentation, family reunion, etc.), I wasn't very honest with you about my feelings/needs. I owe it to you and to our relationship to be really clear. Would you be open to that?

- There has been a lot of tension between us and our departments. When I step back, I think we are about 90 percent on the same page. Can we talk about the 10 percent where we aren't aligned?

Inviting Other Perspectives

Being open to considering other perspectives is an incredible act of collaboration and caring. Often, an unproductive handling of conflict comes from a lack of valuing multiple perspectives. A person sees their perspective as *the* perspective. Considering other perspectives doesn't mean we have to agree with everything we hear, but it does mean you value the other person and the relationship enough to hear it.

When you want to invite perspectives, consider these examples:

- I'm not sure I say out loud enough how much I value you and your perspectives. I'm still trying to make sense of X. How did you see the situation? I'm pushing myself to see this through fresh eyes, and your thoughts would be really helpful.

- I was curious about your experience of that meeting. I got the sense that it took an unexpected turn for both of us, and I didn't leave feeling great about how things ended. I would love to connect and get your perspective.

Effective conversations typically result in clarity, change, and/or closure. Some conversations may have two or more elements present. It can be helpful to think about your ideal goal for the conversation as part of preparing for it. If your conversation was productive, what would the outcome be? Here are a few specific possibilities:

- Increased clarity about the other person, the situation, or yourself.

- Changes in behavior, perception, or understanding.

- Some form of closure. The situation may be fully resolved, maybe you agree to move forward differently, or you may not have a resolution. Regardless of the outcome, you might feel a sense of closure for having the conversation.

Explore

Reflection Guide—Identifying Your Goal For the Conversation

As you think about the conversation you need to have, reflect on the following questions:

1. Are you hoping for changes in clarity or behavior? Or are you hoping for closure?

2. What would it look like to have a positive change in those areas?

3. What would be an ideal outcome of the conversation?

4. What connections can you make between your answers to these questions and the work you've done getting curious about yourself and the other person?

_____

_____

_____

_____

_____

5. Are you having the conversation with the goal of 'winning' or getting your way? How open are you to really engaging with the other person?

_____

_____

_____

_____

_____

_____

Experiment

Practice—Planning Your Opening Statement

The first three minutes of a conversation related to a conflict have the greatest impact on the health of the conversation and ultimately the relationship, according to the Gottman Institute. With that in mind, there are three fundamental truths about starting conversations:

1. Taking the time to plan the start of a conversation dramatically increases the likelihood that the conversation will be successful.

2. Because conversations are so easy to avoid, having some opening lines prepared helps people transition to having the conversation much more easily.

3. People almost always know what they want to say, but often question themselves or get too focused on wordsmithing and continue to avoid the conversation.

Considerations for Your Opening Statements

1. **Ask permission**—"Would you be open to talking about something that has been on my mind related to X?"

2. **Share your intentions**—"I'd like to have an open and honest conversation because I believe it important for us to address."

3. **Express concern**—"I value our relationship and I'd like to talk about something important to me."

4. **Use "We" language**—"We both have a stake in this project, and I'm confident we can find a solution."

5. **Refer to shared goals**—"It's clear we agree on 90 percent, how do we move forward on the final 10 percent?"

As you draft your opening statement, think about the following ingredients:

1. **Match the words and tone**—neither too severe nor too lax based on the situation.

2. **Model the beliefs you want to grow**—this might include acknowledging that it might be challenging, emphasizing that your relationship is bigger than this moment, or providing reassurance that the relationship is strong enough to handle the conversation. Bring curiosity and an interest in exploring perspectives into the conversation from the start.

3. **Be true to yourself**—don't say anything you don't mean.

4. **Get consent for the conversation**—is the other person interested in talking about this? When and how can we both have time and attention for it?

5. Inspired by Kim Scott's *Radical Candor*, **are you clear and demonstrating care for the other person?**

Referring back to the questions in this section, create three different possible opening statements.

Opening Statement 1

_____

_____

_____

_____

Opening Statement 2

Opening Statement 3

As you reflect on your preparation work, what has become clearer for you?

How does this feel different than how you have approached conversations in the past?

Chapter 8

All Together: Freeing the Elephant

When we apply the Curiosity First Approach to process conflict and prepare for a conversation, the odds of success increase dramatically. One common frustration in this work is that people want us to provide them with an exact script of things to say. The beauty of using the Curiosity First Approach is that it tunes you into what is important to you and primes you for curiosity with the other person involved. In getting clear about your needs, values, and experience, you can create a few lines to draw from in the conversation. Perhaps you want to craft and rehearse your opening sentences to invite the conversation and set the stage for success. Perhaps you want to make sure you state your needs in a very clear way and want to write a draft of them to make sure you accomplish that goal.

In addition to preparing for the conversation and being primed for curiosity, there are several productive mindsets and practices for meaningful conversations to consider:

- **Remember that Words Create Worlds**—The words we choose can set or shift the direction of the conversation in significant ways. Are you using words that honor the other person? Are you using words that honor you? Modeling curiosity? Inviting perspective? Promoting partnership? Advocating? Do you know which words resonate with them and which ones don't?

- **Get on the Balcony**—When we are so focused on what is right in front of us, it's easy to miss the larger view. Getting on the balcony is about intentionally expanding that view. From the balcony, we can identify possible themes or patterns. Normalize using the phrase "Getting on the balcony" with your team.

- **Be Invitational**—At the center of this practice is the idea to invite, not to attack, the other person. Our intuitions are very powerful, but they aren't always accurate. We may have a hypothesis or an assumption that needs to be tested. By leaving space to check for understanding, instead of declaring or attacking, we can increase the chances that the dialogue will flow productively. If the other person declines your invitation, do your best to be emphasize that you'll be ready any time if they change their mind.

- **Embrace Silence**—Sitting in silence can serve a lot of purposes. It can allow us to quite literally catch our breath during a tough moment. It can give us time to choose our words intentionally. Silence can also tell us something else is at play or needs to be considered. Resist the temptation to fill any silent moments that occur within a conversation—stop and take a drink, stand up and stretch or go to the window, or even get curious about the silence with some open questions. It's also ok to say something like, "I need a moment to think about that."

- **Seek Self-Awareness**—We can learn an incredible amount about ourselves during challenging conversations. You might experience clarity about your needs, values, or boundaries. You might see something unflattering in yourself that you want to continue to work on. Being in a curious conversation isn't only about curiosity with the others involved; it's also a great opportunity to stay curious with yourself about your patterns and thinking habits.

- **Listen to Learn**—We are wired to listen through a filter of how something matters to us, aligns with our needs, meshes with our experiences, or adds to our responsibilities. Listening to learn requires us to use a different filter: listening to what matters to the other person.

- **Honor Human Complexity**—Remember that everyone coming into the conversation is a complex human being… including you. We have our own individual lived experiences, perspectives, and stress responses. Grace and space can be extremely helpful for all parties involved, so lead the way.

- **Speak and Stand with Courage**—Conversations that matter have some degree of heat. Speaking and standing in the heat takes courage because we must actively choose to breathe, to inquire, to remain open, and to honor our truth.

The Most Common Reactions When Freeing Elephants–and How to Navigate Them

As Viktor Frankl so beautifully said, "Between stimulus and response there is a space. In that space it is our power to choose our response. In our response lies our growth and our freedom." This statement feels incredibly powerful when we consider how often we are on autopilot—so focused on doing and less on thinking.

When you're engaging in a conversation about an elephant, you or the other person may experience any or all of these feelings and behaviors:

- **Being Defensive**—It is completely natural to go into a protection state when we perceive a threat or feel that we are under attack. Sometimes we perceive someone else as being defensive (or in denial or shutting down) and make assumptions about the reasons or the meaning. We owe it to the relationship to get curious about what is really going on. Here are some phrases to go to when it's time to get curious about perceived defensiveness:

    - "I know these types of conversations can feel uncomfortable for all of us. When I see you do X, I wonder if you're shutting down. I know I could be wrong about that. What is true for you right now?"

    - "I can understand why this might be upsetting. Can you help me understand better by sharing your perspective?

- "I didn't expect this conversation to be easy, and I appreciate your willingness to express your concerns."
- "Do you feel like your perspective is being welcomed or judged right now?"
- "Is now a good time to pause? We can revisit this conversation another time if that would be better."
- "I feel like I made a mistake and we're headed in the wrong direction. Can we reset?"
- "Do you feel like you're being heard?"
- "Did I just cross a boundary for you?"

A word of caution about the perception of defensiveness and unchecked bias—women and people of color are far more likely to be perceived as defensive, angry, in denial, or being defiant in conversations even when exhibiting the same behaviors as their white, male counterparts.

- **Anger**—Anger can manifest in many ways. It might look like active aggression, passive aggression, asserting dominance, or making personal attacks. Anger is healthy and acceptable, but these behaviors are unproductive. When you sense that the anger in yourself or the other person is reaching a level where you're struggling to cope in the moment or when unproductive behaviors begin, you might try a sentence like one of these:
    - "It feels like things are getting pretty heated right now. Let's take a break and check in after a day or two has passed."
    - "It's ok that you're angry. It's not ok that you're pounding your fist on the desk and raising your voice."
    - "I know some of this must be hard to hear. Take your time; we can continue when you are ready."

A word of caution about anger—If you are in danger of bodily harm, exit the scenario and seek assistance. No one at work should touch you or threaten you. All of that said, we must be mindful about the layers of complexity here. For example, there is a well-documented history of white women calling security or police when a Black person has done or said something they don't like and used the terminology "unsafe" when it is very likely they were uncomfortable, but not in danger.

- **Dismissive**— Identifying the underlying motivation of someone who is being dismissive might help you better match your response. Sometimes people are dismissive because they don't want the other person to worry. Other times a person is dismissive because they want to minimize the severity of a situation. Another motivation for being dismissive can be not wanting to sit in discomfort with an idea or a situation alongside another person. Here are some possibilities:
    - "This is a big deal for me. Where does it sit in your priorities?"

- "This is really important to me, so I want to make sure you're hearing my perspective."

- "This has been an extremely stressful project, so when I hear you say X, I don't feel like you understand how hard it's been."

- "I understand that you have had a different experience, and I'm asking you to consider that my experience has been different."

A word of caution about being dismissive—If you're on the receiving end of being dismissed, it's normal to feel your anger flare. Feeling minimized and not listened to really kicks our brain into protection mode. Your challenge is to regulate the heat. Turn the heat up or down on the conversation to find a sweet spot where progress can be made.

- **Being Uncomfortable or Awkward**—It's fair to say that feelings of discomfort and awkwardness are extremely common. There might be an increase of silence or non-stop talking. There might be a lot of shifting in the chair or no movement at all. Eye contact may change. To keep the conversation from stalling out, you can try one of these phrases:

  - "I'm glad we are having this conversation. I don't know how you are feeling, but I definitely have some butterflies. I believe that we can get through this together."

  - "I want to try something a little different, and I hope you feel like you can tell me how it goes. I value our partnership so much."

  - "I really appreciate you listening so deeply."

  - "I feel awkward. I'm worried about making mistakes and I'm hoping I can try something with you, and you can tell me how it goes. Does that work for you?"

A word of caution about being uncomfortable or awkward if avoiding or escaping is your default—The most important thing you can do when you're experiencing deep feelings of discomfort or awkwardness is to hold steady. Stay the course of the conversation. Take some breaths, squeeze your coffee mug, ask for some think time, transition to sitting side-by-side or to a walking meeting. Challenge the urge to go silent or abruptly end the conversation. If your natural stress response is kicking in gear, try naming it to de-escalate the feeling.

- **Relief or Appreciation**—Perhaps the most welcome of all the common responses are feelings of relief or appreciation. Conversations are usually more productive and less stressful than we imagine they will be. Sometimes there is relief because of what is accomplished during the conversation, and other times it's a great sense of relief just because we had the conversation. Here are a few phrases you might use:

  - "I'm really glad you brought this up so we could talk about it. Our relationship really matters to me. I feel so much better now."

- "Thank you for having this conversation. I'm so thankful we can talk about the hard stuff." or "I'm so thankful we can talk about little things before they become big things."
- "I'm grateful we can have these kinds of conversations and come out closer on the other side."

A word of caution about being relieved or appreciative—It can be tempting to let a conversation end and move on to the next thing without pausing to express relief or appreciation. We often think about it, but don't say it out loud. It's a great reinforcement of the conversation and the relationship to take the thirty seconds to focus on positive acknowledgement and appreciation. Even better, if you can follow-up after the conversation with things you've done differently because of what they shared, that will further strengthen your relationship.

Explore

Reflection: Productive Mindsets and Practices

Refresh your understanding of the productive mindsets and practices listed below:

- Words create worlds
- Get on the balcony
- Invite, don't demand
- Silence is useful and appropriate
- Seek self-awareness
- Listen to learn
- Honor human complexity
- Speak and stand with courage

1. Which of these do you feel you do well?

_____

_____

_____

_____

2. How do you know? What evidence do you have?

3. Ask people who you know you well. What have they observed?

4. Which of these areas do you need to focus on more intentionally?

5. How do you know? What evidence do you have?

6. Ask people who you know you well. What have they observed?

7. If you could choose just one to focus on, which one do you think would have the biggest impact on improving your conversations?

8. What is one small change you could make that would make a big difference in this area?

_____

_____

_____

_____

_____

_____

A final note from us on this section—we are using *our* words. Do not feel you have to use this exact language, especially if it doesn't fit you or your culture. That said, keep in mind that when you are trying to show up differently than you normally do, it might feel inauthentic. This is to be expected because you are doing something new. The more you practice, the more normal it will feel.

Chapter 9

Receiving the Elephant: The Self-Awareness You Didn't Know You Needed*

***Or thought you already had**

The more power we have, the less self-aware we become. You might have power formally through a title or your place on the organizational chart, but it can also come in the experience or years of service you have within a company. It can also come from having informal power, such as being part of the historically dominant group. Why? One main reason is because fewer people will give you honest feedback. If my manager has enormous control over my wages and opportunities, it only makes sense that I might want to be cautious when giving feedback even when asked to do so.

Another perspective on this issue is that some leaders are uncomfortable with the word "power" and the realities of their positional power. This power dynamic extends to our lives outside of work, too. We see this within parent-child relationships or even between older and younger siblings. If you are in a position of power, it is more likely that people will resist or censor the tough information they want to share—especially if it's about you and your behavior.

The need for a high level of self-awareness applies to all humans—not just those in positions of power. Dr. Tasha Eurich, an organizational psychologist who specializes in self-awareness, found that around 90 percent of people believe they are highly self-aware, but it is closer to 10-15 percent.

Dr. Eurich defines self-awareness through four essential questions:

1. How well do I know myself?
2. How well do I understand why I do what I do?
3. How do I show up? (How do I present myself in a variety of situations?)
4. How do I experience things?

As an added layer of self-awareness, Dr. Eurich challenges us to consider how well we understand how others view us. Do we know how we are perceived by others?

High-performing teams—teams where people accomplish a lot and feel positively connected to each other while they're doing it—have a high degree of psychological safety. Author and Harvard professor Dr. Amy Edmondson notes that psychological safety means that the team creates a safe environment for risk-taking. Dr. Timothy Clark further defines Psychological Safety as a culture where vulnerability is rewarded.

A common misunderstanding is that psychological safety means there is no conflict or discomfort. That absolutely isn't true—the best teams know how to have productive conflict and keep moving forward.

The Power of Trust

Sometimes we encounter people who believe that trust is an "add-on" or "just nice to have" and don't see it as an essential part of how humans work together. Viewing trust as the dessert instead of the main dish leads to stagnation and harm. Without a healthy level of trust, neither giving nor receiving feedback is likely to be successful.

We must remember that:

1. Trust and feedback go hand-in-hand.

2. You don't get to decide if you're trustworthy—other people do.

Elephants and Unconscious Bias

As our colleague and friend Gilmara Vila Nova-Mitchell said, "You can't be a great leader if you can only lead people like you." We couldn't agree more. Effective leaders see the strength in human differences and consciously work to challenge their unconscious and unchecked bias. Effective leaders know that the stakes are higher and some actions may be riskier for some of their team members based on who they are, their life and work experience, what they look like, who they love, or how they worship (or don't worship). Our society has long valued some of us more than others.

When people say, "I don't see gender" or "I don't see race," and they believe it, they are operating with unconscious bias. Sometimes we see these types of comments from folks who boast that they are ruled by logic or data and therefore immune to unconscious bias. Other times it is from people who believe it is impolite to talk about things like race or gender and therefore try to minimize it. People who believe they are acting objectively are more likely to exhibit biased behaviors because they aren't addressing their own biases (it's called the bias blind spot).

Our brains take shortcuts, and some of those shortcuts are called cognitive distortions. We all have unconscious biases, but we can work on checking and challenging those biases daily. Instead of asking ourselves, "Do I have biases?" ask yourself, "How does my focus on what's important to me cause me to miss things that might be important to others? What am I doing to continually see, understand, and challenge my beliefs?"

Explore

1. When is it easy for me to be reflective and practice self-awareness? In which situations? In what contexts? Under what conditions? With which people?

　

2. When is it challenging for me to be reflective and practice self-awareness? In which situations? In what contexts? Under what conditions? With which people?

　

3. What steps am I currently taking to better understand my biases? To challenge my biases?

4. What role do I currently play in creating psychological safety for others in our interactions?

5. How do I know when others feel psychologically safe?

6. What types of behaviors increase psychological safety?

7. What types of behaviors decrease psychological safety?

Experiment

One of the ways we can build trust is by being intentional about talking about the relationship and not just jumping into tasks or staying on auto pilot. Consider having a relationship calibration conversation with someone in your world. This could be with a partner, friend, co-worker, manager. Often, we don't focus on the relationship until there is an issue—and sometimes by then, it is too late.

Take time to explore these questions the next time you are collaborating on a new project, even if you have an existing relationship. People's needs evolve, so don't assume what you or someone needed before is the same this time around. These questions are not exhaustive, just a place to start.

- What should I know about working with you? (Share your needs and preferences as well)
- What would make this a powerful partnership?
- What commitments should we make to set this partnership as a win for both of us?
- How do we want to show up when (not if) we don't show up at our best?
- How will we celebrate?

We had a leader once talk to every team member, peer, and board member using this tool. When they were done, they shared this powerful reflection: "I realized it wasn't just the information I was getting from them that was important. It was that I cared enough to ask and cared enough to listen." Relationships are built one conversation at a time, one moment at a time. If you are not intentionally building trust, you are likely unintentionally losing it.

Receiving the Elephant: Feedback, Intention, and Apologies—Oh My!

A lot of harm can come at the hands of well-intended people. When the pace of work and life is fast and we are navigating so much on a daily basis, we focus more on survival than we do on feedback and reflection. One common trap we see in our work with individual leaders, their teams, and whole organizations is that feedback and reflection are viewed as something you do annually at best. It's often connected only to formal evaluation and compensation instead of an ongoing practice and conversation.

How to Ask for Feedback

It's natural to feel nervous about giving or receiving feedback when we want to keep a relationship strong or to make it stronger. We may have been taught that feedback will risk the relationship with phrases like "kill the messenger." The level of psychological safety and trust you have built with the other person is a huge indicator of success when giving and receiving feedback. This doesn't mean that it will be easy, but it is less likely to cause damage even when it is hard to give or receive.

- **Ask for feedback a lot.** Regularly, once a week, or once a month. Not just once a year during annual reviews.

- **Make sure you're genuinely working on progress** with the last round of feedback before asking for new feedback.

- **Ask for feedback from a variety of different people.** It might be challenging because different people may give you opposing feedback based on their preferences. Distinguish between what is preference and what is consistent.

- **Be as specific as you can about your request for feedback.** Would you like feedback about your behaviors? About how you showed up a specific situation? The more specific you can be, the better your chances of receiving useful feedback.

- **Prime your team to provide feedback.** Sometimes we hear people say that if feedback isn't given in the moment, then it shouldn't be given at all. Although timely feedback is generally more useful, quality feedback is often worth the wait. Let others know what you want feedback on and give them time to reflect. Better yet, name a situation that's coming up and share your need proactively. You might even get feedback that allows you to adjust your behavior or try something different in an upcoming situation.

- **Express gratitude regularly.** Thank people at all stages of the process. Give appreciation for their time. Acknowledge that feedback can be challenging.

- **Remember—all feedback isn't developmental.** Sometimes it's recognizing when someone did something well and they should keep doing it. "I liked it when you…" is also feedback.

Activity—Feedback Plan

1. What do I want to get better at? What do I need feedback about?

   _____
   _____
   _____
   _____
   _____
   _____

2. Who should I ask for feedback? Who would have helpful insight? Whose perspective would I trust? Am I just choosing people who will agree with me? Who should I include that I haven't asked before?

   _____
   _____
   _____
   _____
   _____
   _____

3. What is my specific request? Is there an upcoming situation where my actions could be observed? When and how would I like feedback to be shared?

4. What can I do to make sure my feedback partners can say what they really think? (Pssst...You might have to ask them this question.)

5. Do I need to schedule a time to receive the feedback? Will this happen in person? By phone? Over video? What works best for them and their individual styles?

6. How can I express gratitude at least three times during this process?

_____

_____

_____

_____

_____

How to Receive Feedback

We all claim to want feedback, and in theory, we probably do. Even when we actually want feedback or see it as essential to our growth, receiving feedback can be extremely uncomfortable. Let's face it: many of us think we're better at feedback than we are. As managers of people, we have to be aware that research, in fact, has shown that having more power correlates to having less self-awareness. It's also true that it's a very human response for our brains to spend more energy protecting us from pain than moving to pleasure—which could be part of the reason why, when we could use feedback-filled moments to build trust, we often default to responding from a place of protection instead of partnering.

Partnering around feedback is a core component of building psychological safety in your organization, which research shows us is absolutely critical in building trust among high-performing teams. The bottom line is that more trust equals more psychological safety, and more psychological safety equals more effective teams.

So, where does feedback come in? Consider this: when we're getting feedback from a 360, an engagement survey or in-person conversation, what we observe is that leaders tend to focus more on the content of the feedback and less on the intentionality of the response to the feedback. The reality is that our response actually signals an answer to a bigger, more human question behind the comments: "Can I trust you or not?"

And, because we're human too, our response to feedback often casts doubt about our trustworthiness. Too often, in our work with over 500 corporate clients over the years, we've seen deflection play out in the following patterns. As you read, we invite you to resist the urge to assume you've never done them. Instead, try to ask yourself when you might have, whether from a place of protection or an unconscious reaction:

1. **Defensive Repositioning**—Shifting focus from reflecting to deflecting by saying or thinking some version of, "I guess you just can't say anything these days."

2. **Finger Pointing**—Shifting focus from reflecting to attacking by saying or thinking some version of, "You think I need to work on X? THEY need to work on X!"

3. **Mystified Denying**—Shifting focus from reflecting to feigning ignorance by saying or thinking some version of, "I just don't understand where this feedback could be coming from. I guess we'll never know . . . "

4. **Dismissive Undermining**—Shifting focus from reflecting to playing passive-aggressive detective by saying or thinking some version of, "I'm pretty sure I know who said this, and you can never make them happy. What do they even know about X, anyway?"

5. **Manipulative Appeasing**—Shifting focus from reflecting to pacifying by saying or thinking some version of, "I'm just going to tell them what they want to hear so this gets over quickly."

Explore

1. Which of the common responses resonates the most?

2. Think about a time you received feedback well, even when it might have felt uncomfortable. What did the other person do that made it easier to receive? What did you do? What didn't you do? What might you be able to repeat from that experience in the future?

Rules for Receiving Feedback

The more power, either formal or informal, you have in a situation or relationship, the more the other person will watch how you receive feedback—whether you asked for it or not. The ways you respond will determine whether they'll do it again.

- **Acknowledge the feedback**—Try a sentence like, "Thank you for sharing your perspective."

- **Give yourself space to process**—Take a breath and a step back. Try a sentence like, "This is tough for me to hear because this isn't how I want to show up," or "I hadn't thought of it that way. I appreciate that you trusted me to share your experience."

- **Follow up**—One of the fastest ways to damage trust is to request feedback and then do absolutely nothing with it. A great way to enhance trust is to follow up on the feedback you receive. Try a sentence like, "I wanted to follow up about the feedback you gave me about X. I appreciate you for drawing my attention to it because that is something I've been working on for a while. During our next meeting, I'm going to try Y instead of X." Even better, share the feedback to a group: "Someone shared that this was their experience of me. That's not how I want to show up, so I'm going to try X. I'd appreciate your help if you see me slipping."

- **Consider the feedback**—Not all feedback you receive will feel relevant or appropriate to you or your goals. We recommend two reflection questions before you consider whether to act on the feedback or how to prioritize it:

    a. "What might be true about this that I haven't considered?"

    b. "What might I be doing or not doing that is giving them that perception?"

    c. "What behaviors could change that perception?"

- **Express gratitude**—Assuming the feedback was helpful or well-intended, express gratitude to the person. Try a sentence like, "Thank you again. When you give me feedback, you're signaling that you trust that I can receive it and do better. I appreciate it."

Feedback that isn't specific and behaviorally driven can feel abusive, ill-intended, or mocking. This is not feedback. It's bias or abuse. There are two podcasts we love that explore the challenges and best practices with feedback. The first is Fixable, hosted by Dr. Francis Frei and Dr. Anne Morriss. The second podcast is Real As Feedback, hosted by Jackye Clayton, Kim Scott, and Kieran Snyder.

Experiment

Imagine how impactful it could be for you and the people in your life if you asked them both what you do well and what you could do differently to show up more powerfully for them.

Take a few minutes to think how you might respond to feedback differently given your journey in this workbook.

1. I will likely receive feedback soon on...

2. What's the current script in your mind? What would you usually say or do when you receive feedback?

3. What specifically do you like to try to do differently? (Psst—Take some hints from the five steps above.)

4. What specifically would you like to say the next time you receive feedback? Take a moment to write a new script for your brain to have at the ready. (Psst—Take some hints from the five steps above.)

___

Here is one of our favorite sets of questions to keep things simple, short, and specific:

1. What should I continue doing or amplify that is positively impacting our relationship?

___

2. What should I consider doing new or differently to have a more positive impact on our relationship?

___

Anytime we are asking for feedback, we want to be sure to thank the person for their time, thoughtfulness, and likely, risk. Don't just become good at asking for feedback; become great at acting on what you hear.

When—And How—to Apologize

When done well, apologies are one of the most powerful ways to build trust and strengthen relationships. Let's go through the key components of an appropriate apology.

Name the situation—Try a sentence like, "I want to apologize for (insert your action here) yesterday."

Own the impact—Try a sentence like, "I want to apologize for the impact that had on you and for shutting down your ideas in front of the group."

Reinforce the value of the relationship—Try a sentence like, "Our partnership is incredibly important to me, and you deserved better than that."

Leave intention out—This is so challenging because our intention often doesn't line up with our impact. You should absolutely reflect your intentions and the factors that created the disconnect between your good intentions and your actual impact, but that shouldn't be included in your apology. It can sound like an excuse, like, "but this is why I was right to do it."

Commit to doing things differently—After you've had some time to cool off, regroup, and apologize, it's time to commit to doing things differently. This might mean learning new strategies and might mean unlearning old habits. After you have some clarity, you can share these insights if it's appropriate to do so. Try a sentence like, "I realized that I need to get better at X, so I've started…"

Let's put the steps together now. Your apology might sound like this:

"I want to apologize for talking over you and criticizing your ideas in the meeting yesterday. I acknowledge the impact that had on you and the dynamic of the whole group after I shut down your ideas. I value you and your ideas, and you deserve to be heard. I'm sorry I showed up that way."

Experiment

Every moment spent planning a conversation—especially one that requires an apology—will increase the likelihood the conversation will be successful. Use the template below to map out your apology.

Name the situation—be as specific as you can.

For example, *"I want to apologize for my tone of voice in the meeting yesterday."*

_____
_____
_____
_____
_____
_____
_____

Own the impact—communicate that you understand your actions impacted the other person, the situation, or the group.

For example, *"After the meeting ended, I realized how my tone negatively impacted the group and the shut down the brainstorming session."*

_____
_____
_____
_____
_____
_____
_____

Reinforce the value of the relationship—Many people struggle with this step because it requires an element of vulnerability, but sharing how much you value the relationship is a critical step. That said, don't say anything you don't mean.

For example, *"I have tremendous respect for you. I value your innovative mind and you're a huge asset to the team."*

_____

_____

_____

_____

_____

_____

Commit to doing things differently—If you have considered something you will do differently in the future, include that in your apology. Make sure that you aren't committing to something you do not truly want to do because this can negatively impact trust.

For example, *"The next time I feel so agitated before the meeting starts, I will take a few minutes to collect myself before I come in to join the team."*

_____

_____

_____

_____

_____

_____

Chapter 11

When Freeing the Elephant Goes Differently than We'd Hoped

Unwillingness is usually the largest barrier to resolving a conflict. In this work, we've seen firsthand that sometimes even skillful attempts at freeing elephants don't yield the outcomes we wanted. The biggest indicator that the conflict won't be resolved is when someone expresses an unwillingness to work toward resolving it. There are times that people aren't ready yet and might need time, space, and the invitation to return to the conversation. However, there are times that people do not want to resolve a conflict. They might have decided that the effort required to resolve the conflict doesn't feel worth it or that the damage done was too severe. The power dynamic present in a relationship can add additional complication to resolving conflicts.

If you find yourself in a situation that isn't moving forward, you might want to consider the following strategies:

1. **Seek to understand the resistance—when applicable.** It's important to remember that seeking to understand doesn't mean you have to agree or that you need to surrender your values, beliefs, or needs. Often our resistance is rooted in a sense of loss—loss of power, loss of control, and/or loss of comfort or familiarity.

2. **Accept the reality.** There are many factors that contribute to your willingness to accept and to stay in a situation that isn't likely to be resolved. We often see people who decide to tolerate difficult situations because there aren't good job prospects at the time or in their area. Others have been caring for family members and needed the financial security the job provided. If you choose to stay in a situation with a significant conflict that cannot be resolved and it is affecting your mental health, consider reaching out to a counselor or mental health professional to work to safeguard your mental health until you are able to leave the situation.

3. **Choose your own path.** We recommend the work of Marshall Goldsmith, author and coach, who suggests there are three basic choices for how to respond to a situation, "Accept, Adjust, or Avoid." Acceptance doesn't mean resignation or resentment, but an understanding and acceptance of the situation. Adjust might look like adjusting your perspective, the situation, how you work together, etc. You are making an intentional choice of change to be able to navigate the situation more effectively for you. Finally, Goldsmith's

"Avoid" may look like minimizing time with that person or leaving a situation/job. In our eyes, all three are valid choices based on the circumstances.

4. **Know when to leave.** Throughout this book—and in this chapter specifically—we want to be very explicit that we are not in any way suggesting that self-care, curiosity, or intentionality can remove the harm of working or being in a toxic or abusive situation. Listen to yourself. Believe in yourself. Do what is best for you.

Explore

Questions to ask yourself when deciding to address a stubborn or potentially violent (physically or emotionally) situation:

1. How is my body reacting? When? With whom?

2. What types of risk are involved?

3. Is this situation impacting my health (physical, mental, or social)? In what ways? How often?

4. What is the likelihood of retaliation?

5. What is at stake if I continue to address it?

6. What is at stake if I stop trying to address it?

7. Is my job at stake?

8. Am I willing to risk being fired?

9. Am I worried about bodily harm?

Strategies for Taking Care of Yourself
Seek Allies

Explore—Who is in my corner? Who do I trust? Who else would listen and ensure confidentiality?

_____
_____
_____
_____
_____
_____
_____

Experiment—Who else might I connect with to support me during this challenge? Is there a mentor I could reach out to? A friend of a friend who has been through a similar situation? An online support group?

_____
_____
_____
_____
_____
_____
_____

Get Your Bucket Filled Elsewhere

Explore—What types of things belong in my self-care manual or playbook? Who am I excited to be around? What types of activities leave me feeling energized? What types of activities leave me feeling calm? What is something new I have wanted to try and haven't yet? What types of causes or organizations might feel good to be involved with?

_____

Experiment—What can I try that I haven't tried before or for a while? What is one thing I can try today? This week?

_____

Seek Help

Explore—Which professionals (professional counselor, coach, physician) are currently in my life who might serve as a good support? Am I able to meet more regularly in person or virtually? What virtual options exist? What can I financially afford?

_____

_____

_____

_____

_____

_____

_____

Experiment—Reach out to people you trust to ask for recommendations or referrals to good providers. It's ok to meet with a provider and then try a new one. Find someone you connect with.

_____

_____

_____

_____

_____

_____

_____

Set Boundaries

Explore—Where are my current boundaries set? Which ones are working well? Which ones aren't serving me? What would success look like in setting healthier boundaries?

_____
_____
_____
_____
_____
_____
_____
_____

Experiment—What can I try? Can I unplug from technology at a certain time each day? Can I try meditation or other mindfulness practices? Can I work to mentally unplug at a certain point on my commute home?

_____
_____
_____
_____
_____
_____
_____
_____

(**Teresa Tip:** I found success with this by setting up a ritual on my evening commute while surviving in a toxic work environment. I crossed over a bridge, removed my employee badge, and then drank some water. When I got home, I immediately changed out of my work clothes. I narrowed my work clothes down to just a handful of pieces that I visualized being like armor and kept them in a small, but separate spot in the closet. I also started leaving my comfortable clothes out on the bed or in the bathroom, so they were waiting for me. It always felt like a gift at the end of a miserable day. This ritual might resonate with you and it might not. Either way is ok. Our brain loves routines. Initially, I had a hard time relaxing even after I had changed clothes, but I kept on with it and after a couple of weeks, I could start to feel myself relax even as I approached the bridge. Experiment with your own routines and rituals. They don't have to make sense to other people to work well for you.)

Chapter 12

Ready, Set, Act!

One of our core principles is that theory is great, but tools are better. In that spirit, here are ten specific ways you can introduce the concept of elephants to your team:

1. **Have a conversation about an elephant that is not specific to your organization.** If it feels too risky to talk about an elephant that is impacting the team, share a story about an elephant that was freed in another group. Help people get familiar with the language of elephants and how to utilize curiosity with one another.

2. **Share a monthly email where you explore elephants.** Celebrate team members who have gotten curious in tough situations or shared observations that have shifted the team's thinking. Recognize elephants that were freed and wish them well. Share sample language that people can use right away.

3. **Bring an actual elephant to meetings.** Many teams we work with started bringing a stuffed elephant, a picture of an elephant, or a copy of *Don't Feed the Elephants!* to their meetings. The visual reminders often help the team stay connected to the goal of communicating with clarity and curiosity.

4. **Keep a visual anchor in your office.** What we talk about with regularity creates our culture, which creates our reality. Having a visual reminder of our goal—called a visual anchor—can be helpful in helping you keep your focus top of mind. Sarah likes to wear an elephant necklace when she's working with teams. Other leaders we have served place a small elephant near their computer or office table. Our hybrid friends often put sticky note reminders around their monitors.

5. **Create an award.** One of our clients created an "elephant wrangler" award for team members who have done the tough work of identifying and freeing elephants. Recognizing and celebrating when we step into the hard work when it would be easier to perpetuate avoidance is a great way to encourage more of the behavior you want to see. Pay attention to who submits award nominations, who receives them, and who doesn't. Awards usually reflect your organizations' biases.

6. **Form a group of elephant champions.** This can be a group dedicated to sharing micro-learnings on a weekly or monthly basis to keep the momentum going. Elephant champions might also serve as coaches for those who are ready to have conversations but need a thinking partner to get started.

7. **Create an unexpected experience.** Sarah and a group of elephant champions she worked with brought a balloon sculptor to their office to interact with the staff. The sense of playfulness and curiosity made for a fantastic conversation starter about curiosity in their workshop later in the day. You might also consider something like a going away party for an elephant that has been freed—if you ask us, cake is always a good idea. For our virtual or hybrid teams, we often send elephant themed gift boxes that can be opened and enjoyed together online.

8. **Play the (curious) questions only game.** Many of our ideas are rooted in assumptions. To disrupt the assumption-driven default we can fall into, it can help to ask curious questions. Set a time for five to ten minutes and say, "Let's see how many questions we can come up with related to this challenge. No solutions, No answers. No discrediting other comments or questions. Just asking questions." Curious questions might sound like this, "What else could we try?" "What does success look like?" "How do we know that X and Y are connected?" "What else might be true?" "How might assumptions about X be driving our thinking about Y?" "What don't we know about this situation?"

9. **Just ask one big, curious question.** A thoughtful, curious question is the gateway to possibility. You can use any of the questions above and your one, big curious question. After you ask it, let it breathe. Be comfortable sitting in silence. Take a drink of water. Let everyone know it's ok to sit with the question.

10. **Normalize and encourage elephant prevention.** The more we can foresee elephant-causing situations and call attention to them in the moment, the easier we can prevent them from moving into our offices and homes. It takes much less effort to prevent elephants and much more to free them. Celebrate proactive elephant prevention conversations.

Explore

1. Which of the ideas in this chapter might be a fit for you and your team? Which ones might feel safest? Which ones might feel risky?

2. What ideas do you have for exploring the topic of elephants within your organization?

3. What support do you have? What resources are currently available? What resources might you be able to get?

4. What can you do new or differently today to encourage a culture of curiosity? How will you observe and monitor changes in yourself and others?

Experiment

- Choose one of the ideas above and test it out with your team. Invite people to share observations, shifts in thinking, and feedback to evolve the idea to better fit your group.

- Create an informal award or recognition for elephant prevention and elephant freeing. Invite others to shine a light on those behaviors—provide fun incentives like a traveling trophy, a treat the person enjoys, or a Wordle that could be displayed at their desk or used as a virtual background for online meetings. Remember, the incentives should fit the way people like to be recognized. For some, a boisterous cheer and high-five would be bucket-fulling, but for others, a low-key sticky note at their desk or a card received in the mail would be more meaningful.

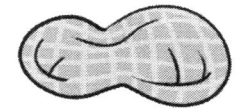

Closing Thoughts

As we wrap up our journey together, we hope this workbook has served as a valuable companion in helping you explore your relationship with conflict avoidance. Our goal is that you have not only deepened your understanding but have also gained practical strategies to begin taking small, meaningful steps towards more courageous conversations.

We understand that engaging in these conversations may never feel fully comfortable, but it's our hope that you now feel better equipped and braver when facing them. Even when difficult, these conversations can lead to stronger connections, deeper trust, and healthier relationships.

Remember, this is a journey, not a destination. Every conversation you have with yourself and others is a step forward. We have seen firsthand how these tools have helped others as well as ourselves. Cheers to conversations that have greater curiosity, compassion, and candor. Thank you for letting us to be a part of your journey towards having conversations that truly matter.

Sarah and Teresa

Made in the USA
Columbia, SC
29 January 2025